Earth's Natural Resources

by Raquel Martin

PEARSON
Scott
Foresman

DK

What Resources Are

Resources are materials that help meet the needs of living things. **Natural resources** are important materials from Earth that living things need.

Trees are one example of a natural resource. Trees give people the material needed to make many things. Wood is used to make lumber for building homes. Wood is also used to make pencils and even paper.

Some other natural resources are water, soil, air, and sunlight. All these resources come straight from nature. These natural resources are used every day. You are always breathing air. You always need to drink water. Plants and trees need sunlight, soil, water, and air to grow.

What natural resources is this farm using to grow crops?

Crops ready for harvesting   **Plowed field ready for planting**

Resources We Can Replace

Some natural resources can be easily replaced. These are called **renewable resources.** We often plant new trees to replace the ones we cut down. If we eat all the crops that farmers grow one year, more can be planted the next year.

Resources We Cannot Replace

There are some natural resources that we cannot make again. Earth can run out of many resources. Once we use them up, they are gone. These resources are called **nonrenewable resources.**

Many nonrenewable resources are used for very important tasks. A lot of them, such as natural gas, oil, and coal, are used as fuel. Once these resources are used up, we cannot make any more of them.

Some resources are always available on Earth. Sunlight, air, and water cannot be used up.

Iron

Coal

Oil

Protecting Natural Resources

It is important to find ways to save our natural resources. We do not want to use them all up. People have learned how important it is to care for our natural resources. By doing that, we will have them in the future.

Conservation is the careful use of natural resources so they are not wasted or used up. When you practice conservation, you use only what you need. You also make sure not to waste anything.

Turning the lights off when you leave the room and turning off the water while you brush your teeth help conserve electricity and water.

This new car runs on electricity and gasoline. It creates less air pollution than old cars, which use up a lot of gasoline.

There are many ways people conserve resources. Car companies are making new cars that run on both electricity and gasoline. They are also changing the way cars that use gasoline work. Now some cars use less. This helps conserve gasoline. Gasoline is a nonrenewable resource. Using less gas also causes less air pollution. This way, air can stay clean for longer. But the easiest way to use less gasoline is to take fewer trips in the car.

Sometimes conserving resources means using a little less of something. Next time you buy something at the store, you could use your backpack to carry it home instead of taking a new paper bag. This way, fewer paper bags are used. Then fewer trees need to be cut down to make them. Ask your mom or dad to bring back the bags they use at the grocery store each time they go. This saves paper too.

Take old paper or plastic bags, or your own backpack, when you go shopping.

Planting trees by the side of a river protects its banks.

One way to help conserve water and keep
it clean is to plant trees along riverbanks.
Tree roots grow deep into the moist soil along
a riverbank. This makes it harder for soil to
wear away in the wind or rain. The trees
also help keep soil from sliding down into
the water. This kind of conservation helps
keep water clean. It also adds more trees
to Earth. It keeps the soil healthy too. Clean
water and soil are very important to animals
that make their homes near rivers.

What We Do with Trash

We make many things out of natural resources. Aluminum cans, plastic bags, newspapers, aluminum foil, and glass bottles are all made from natural resources. Many of these things are used every day. What happens to them after we use them? We throw them out in the trash. But where does all our trash go?

We bury a lot of our trash in landfills. A landfill is a place where a giant hole is dug into the ground and covered with a liner. Our trash is put on top of the liner so it does not sink into the soil. Our trash never really goes away, and we are running out of places to bury it. Some places have tried burning trash instead. But burning trash can cause air pollution.

Where does your trash go? Can you think of ways to cut down on the amount of trash that you make?

Ways to Use Resources Again

A different way to solve our trash problem is to make less trash. You can help do this every day. Maybe you could use empty jars to hold things such as pens and pencils. Or when you have finished drinking a can of juice, do not throw it in the trash. Recycle it.

When we **recycle** something, it gets changed so we can use it again. For example, you can recycle your plastic juice containers. They can go to a recycling center. There they might be made into plastic parts that will be put in a new computer!

There are separate recycling bins for paper, glass, aluminum, and plastic.

Used aluminum foil

Old aluminum is made into new aluminum cans.

Old aluminum can

New aluminum can

Recycling is the reason people put their trash into different piles. Newspapers get recycled. Plastic, glass, and aluminum get recycled too. These things do not go to a landfill and take up space. They go to a recycling center.

When an aluminum can goes to a recycling center, it is chopped into little pieces. Very hot air takes any paint off the metal scraps. Then these scraps are melted in an even hotter furnace. The melted aluminum is poured into molds, and new cans are made. These cans may end up back at the recycling center once they've been used again.

How to Recycle

People have been recycling for a long time. Your parents probably do it, and you can too. When you help with the shopping, you can tell your parents that it is a good idea to pick things with a recycling symbol on the package. This means that the box, jar, or can that the food comes in was made from recycled materials. Even your clothing can be made from recycled material. Everything from wrapping paper to car tires can be made from recycled goods today.

Look for recycling symbols such as this one when you are shopping.

Remember the three Rs. *Reduce* the amount of natural resources you use and the amount of trash you create. *Reuse* as many things as you can. *Recycle* all the things that you can. This way, you are really helping the planet.

Collect things made of plastic, glass, paper, and aluminum. All these things can be recycled.

Reduce your trash. Reuse or recycle as many things as possible.

Glossary

conservation   protecting natural resources from being used up or wasted

natural resources   materials supplied by nature that living things need

nonrenewable resources   natural resources that cannot be replaced

recycle   to change or treat something so that it can be used again

renewable resources   natural resources that can be replaced